Collins

Revised Edition

1

EXPEDITIONS

A Course in Environmental Studies

Series Editor
Padmini Sriraman

Student + Teacher		Teacher-only	
a animations	**ia** activities	**lp** lesson plans	**tn** teacher's notes
ilt instructor-led tutorials	**w** worksheets	**w** worksheets	**ak** answer keys
g games	**v** videos		
audio			

Preface

If I cannot learn the way you teach, teach the way I can learn.

Expeditions (Revised Edition) is a comprehensive course in Environmental Studies and Social Studies for the primary and middle school. This series for classes 1 to 8 has been designed taking into account the multidisciplinary nature of Environmental Studies and Social Studies. Following an interactive approach, the series caters to the young learners through inferential and experiential tasks, and stimulating content. The need for sustainable development holds the key to the future of mankind and young learners need to be sensitized to it through a gradual study to build environmental and social awareness.

Expeditions (Revised Edition) is based on the underlying principle of the National Curriculum Framework that every learner can learn. This series maximizes opportunities to learn through its wide variety of tasks and facilitates easy learning and comprehension of the concepts at the primary level. Multiple intelligence-based tasks cater to the needs of all learners. With a learner-centric approach for effective teaching and learning in the classroom, the series promotes experiential learning. Course materials are drawn from the curriculum and provide examples from real-life situations to foster knowledge building and understanding. The series provides ample scope for the learners to observe, reflect, hone their thinking skills and develop effective communication skills. Learners are guided to look at the environment in a holistic manner and see the underlying unity in the physical and social environment.

Key Features

- **Take off** assesses the prior knowledge of the learners.
- **Warm up** has pre-reading tasks for discovery-based learning where learners can infer and relate to the topic.
- **Fact quest** provides interesting titbits of information and **Find out** tasks encourage referencing skills.
- **Do it yourself** contains application-based activities for experiential learning.
- **Eco feat** sensitizes learners towards conservation of the environment.
- **Recall** provides mind maps and flowcharts to reinforce learning.
- **Work out** at the end of the units facilitate understanding, recall and reinforcement, and assessment.
- **Think** focuses on Higher Order Thinking Skills.
- **Life Skills and Values** equips learners with the basic skills they need to excel in life and helps to build the right attitudes and values in learners.
- **Enjoy** has varied creative tasks.
- **Fun Time** has varied tasks for game-based learning.
- **Outline maps** are given for map practice.

The comprehensive teacher's resource materials are aimed at facilitating teaching and assessment. Feedback and suggestions to improve the course further are welcome.

Key Features

Take off

- The Frigid Zone is the .... heat zone of the Earth.
- The areas in the Frigid Zone remain covered by .... most of the time.

Assesses the prior knowledge of the learners

Warm up

Which landform can be seen in the picture? What kind of climate does this region experience?

Has warm-up tasks that initiates the learners into the topic and help them relate to it

Fact quest

The word 'hello' was used to answer the first telephone call.

Provides interesting titbits of information

Recall

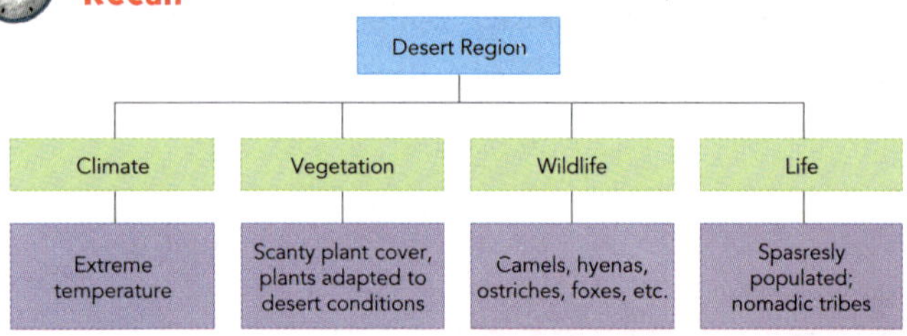

Recall

- Many people help us at home, in school and in the neighbourhood.
- We should be thankful to them and treat them with respect.

Is a ready reckoner of the chapter

Find out

Why is there a huge difference between day and night temperatures in hot deserts?

Tasks to encourage referencing skills

Eco feat

We should keep plants near windows and in balconies as they make the air clean.

Sensitizes learners towards conservation of environment

Do it yourself

Read this rhyme and answer the questions.

Cobbler, Cobbler, what do you do?
I mend your shoes and polish them too.
Gardener, Gardener, what do you do?
I help keep your garden green under the sky so blue.
Barber, Barber, what do you do?
I cut your hair and style it too.

1. What does a cobbler use to polish our shoes?
2. What does the gardener use to keep our garden beautiful?
3. What does a barber use to cut our hair?

Activities for learners to attempt on their own

Work out

A. Fill in the blanks with the correct answers.

1. A .... makes chairs for us.
   a. gardener b. carpenter
2. A .... mends our shoes.
   a. cobbler b. pilot

Reinforces learning and facilitates assessment

Think

Imagine that the community helper who cleans your neighbourhood does not come for a week. What do you think will happen?

Focuses on Higher Order Thinking Skills

Life Skills and Values

Your gardener steps on a spade and cuts his foot while working. What would you do? Tick (✓) the correct option.

1. Run inside your house for help. ☐
2. Bring the first-aid kit. ☐
3. Stand there and watch. ☐

Equips learners with the basic skills they need to excel in life

Enjoy

Make a list of people who help you at home like the house helper, milkman, gardener, cook, guard and others. Take a chart paper and draw smiling faces on it. Colour them and cut them out with the help of an adult. Give these to the helpers to thank them for their help.

Has varied creative tasks

WORKSHEET

Worksheet (Chapters 13-16)

A. Fill in the blanks.

1. We get .... and .... from animals.
2. Drinking .... water will make us sick.
3. We need .... to breathe and live.
4. .... have a strong, thick stem called trunk.
5. The Sun is high in the sky in the ....

Facilitate assessment and evaluation

Web link

For more information, watch this documentary by BBC Hindi:

https://www.youtube.com/watch?v=2jQ1txKwuWU

Last accessed on 30 September, 2019

Encourage extended learning

FUN TIME

Look at the untidy room. Clean the room by joining things to their proper places in the second picture. One has been done for you.

Fun Time has varied tasks for game-based learning.

Outline maps are given for map practice

Contents

1 Meet Me

Take off

- I am a .... (boy/girl).
- My name is ....
- My birthday is on ....
- I am .... years old.

Warm up

Look at old photographs of yourself as a baby to see how much you have grown.

Hello, I am Rajul. I am a boy. I am five years old. Jojo is my dog. I like to play with him every day.

▲ Playing with my dog

I have many friends at school. They are Bina, Rehan and Jaskirat. We call Jaskirat, Jassi. It is her **nickname**.

Do you have a nickname too?

My friends and I study together. We also enjoy playing games.

Fact quest

The word 'hello' was used to answer the first telephone call.

▲ Playing with my friends

---

nickname: pet name of people

Have you seen children wearing cards in school?

These cards are called **identity cards**. The card tells us a few things about the person wearing it, such as his or her name, class and birthday.

Do it yourself

Complete the identity card.

School Name: ....

SCHOOL IDENTITY CARD

Paste photograph here

Class: .... Roll No: ....

Name: ....

Date of Birth: ....

Find out

Who else carries an identity card in your family?

Eco feat

Use blank pages from old notebooks for drawing.

Things we like to do

I like to cycle and play with my toys.
I also like to watch television.

The things that we enjoy the most are our **favourite** things. I like drawing in my free time. It is my **hobby**.

▲ A drawing I made of my family

▲ Playing with my toys

▲ Dancing

▲ Singing

favourite: something liked more than others of the same kind; **hobby:** something one likes to do in one's free time

List your favourite things in the table.

Game	Hobby	Food	Dress	Book

Recall

- Friends study and play together and help each other.
- The things we enjoy doing the most are our favourite things.
- A hobby is something we like to do in our free time.

Work out

A. Underline the correct answer.

1. Friends play together/alone.
2. A pet name is/is not a nickname.
3. Our hobbies are the things we like to do during night/our free time.
4. The things that we enjoy the least/most are our favourite things.

B. Join the numbers to complete the picture and colour it.

C. Write Yes or No.

1. I wear glasses. ....
2. I have a nickname. ....
3. I have a hobby. ....
4. I have curly hair. ....

Think

Rajul greets everyone by saying 'hello'. Think of three other words you can use to greet people.

Life Skills and Values

What makes you happy or sad? Write H for happy and S for sad next to the phrases.

1. Having a toothache ....
2. Getting wet in the rain ....
3. Being hugged ....
4. Eating a chocolate ....

Enjoy

Make a card for your friend.

1. Take a drawing sheet and cut it from the top corners.
2. Ask an adult to help you make a hole in the top.
3. Draw something that you think your friend will like on the card.
4. Tie a ribbon around the hole and gift it to your friend.

2 Our Body

Take off

- I like to ....
- I use my .... to draw.

Warm up

Which part of your body helps you to see things?

Our body helps us do many things. It has many parts. Each part of the body is important. Let us learn about our body.

Look at the pictures and tell the body parts that are being used to do these actions.

▲ Eating

▲ Playing ball

▲ Running

▲ Reading

Each part of our body is useful. We use different parts of our body to carry out different actions. We breathe through our nose. We walk and jump using our legs. We eat using our hands.

Look at the picture and read aloud the names of the body parts with your teacher.

▲ Parts of the body

Find out

How many body parts do we have in pairs?

Sense Organs

We can see, hear, taste, smell and feel. Our eyes, ears, tongue, nose and skin help us do these things. These are called **sense organs**.

Fact quest

Our body prevents us from getting hurt. Our eyes close when we look at the Sun or when it is windy.

Write the names of the sense organs being used to do these actions.

We **see** with our ....

We **hear** with our ....

We **taste** with our ....

sense organs: parts of the body that help us to see, hear, taste, smell and touch

We **smell** with our ....

We **feel** with our ....

Do it yourself

Circle the names of sense organs in yellow and other body parts in green.

eyes	legs	chin	tongue	head
ears	hands	skin	nose	lips

Recall

- Our body helps us do many things.
- Each part of our body is useful.
- Our body has five sense organs.

Work out

A. Colour the boxes green if you can do these tasks.

1. Leap like a frog ☐
2. Fly like a bird ☐
3. Write with your left hand ☐
4. Stand on one foot for 15 seconds ☐

B. Write T for true and F for false.

1. We have three eyes. ☐
2. We have one head. ☐
3. We have four legs. ☐
4. We have two hands. ☐

C. Write which body part or parts would you use to do these actions.

1. Kick a ball .... 3. Write and draw ....

2. Eat food .... 4. Listen to music ....

Think

Observe a bird, dog, cat and an ant. Think and say which part of the body these animals use to move.

Life Skills and Values

Find out which part of the body controls all the other body parts.

Enjoy

Make a finger painting!

- You will require a sheet of paper, paint and other colours.
- Put your thumb in paint.
- Press it on a sheet of paper.
- Do this four times in a circular shape to print four thumb prints.
- Colour the centre yellow.
- You have drawn a flower which you can show to your friends.

3 Healthy and Clean

Take off

- I bathe daily in the .... (morning/evening).
- I wear .... (clean/dirty) clothes and keep my hair combed.

Warm up

How many times in a day do you wash your hands?

We should take care of our body as it helps us to do different activities. We should keep our body **healthy** and clean. This **prevents** us from falling sick.

Healthy Habits

Doing something daily or often forms a **habit**. We should have healthy habits.

- Eat food that gives us **energy** and keeps our body fit.
- Always drink clean water.
- **Exercise** regularly to stay fit and healthy.
- Sleep on time and wake up early.
- Breathe in fresh air.

▲ Exercise regularly

Fact quest

Fingernails grow faster than toenails.

healthy: fit; in a good condition; **prevents:** stops something from happening; **energy:** strength to work; **exercise:** activity done to stay healthy

Stay Clean

Keeping our body clean keeps us in good health.

We should do the following activities to keep ourselves clean.

Bathe daily.

Brush our teeth twice daily.

Trim our nails regularly.

Comb our hair neatly.

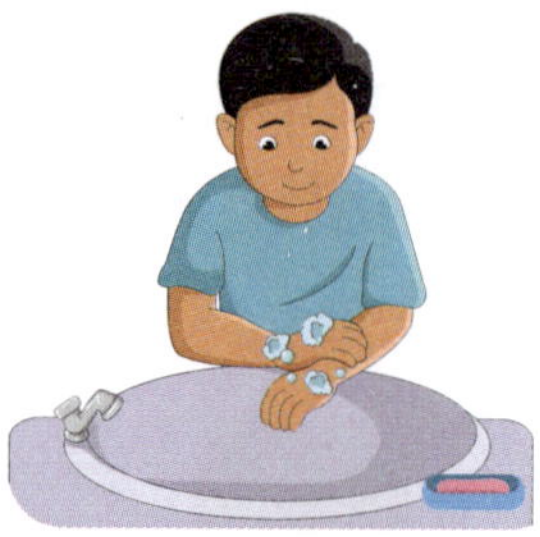

Wash our hands before and after eating food.

Find out

Why should we clean our tongue while brushing teeth?

Do it yourself

Name these four things we use to take care of our body.

....

Remember, a healthy body is a **valuable** gift. We should look after it.

valuable: something useful and important

Recall

- We should take care of our body.
- We should have healthy habits.
- We should eat food that gives us energy and drink clean water.
- We should exercise regularly.
- We should keep our body clean.

Work out

A. Write T for true and F for false.

1. It is not important to bathe daily. ☐
2. We should wash our hands before and after eating food. ☐
3. We should brush our teeth twice a week. ☐
4. We should comb our hair neatly. ☐

B. Look at some activities you do in the morning. Number them in the correct order.

 ☐  ☐  ☐  ☐

C. Choose the correct word from the box and fill in the blanks.

clean	exercise	sleep	twice	energy

1. We must keep our body ....
2. We should .... on time to give rest to our body.

3. We should .... daily to stay fit.
4. We should eat food that gives us ....
5. We should brush our teeth .... daily.

Think

Shreya said, 'It's not important to play and exercise daily.' Is Shreya right? Give reasons for your answer.

Life Skills and Values

You woke up late. It is time to go to school. What would you do?

1. Skip brushing teeth ☐
2. Eat breakfast slowly ☐
3. Skip your exercise ☐
4. Have a quick bath ☐

Enjoy

On a sheet of paper, make a list of the things you need to do to keep your body healthy.

Decorate the sheet by stamping it using a ladies' finger dipped in paint. Display it on the bulletin board.

4 Family

Take off

- I live with my ....
- I have a younger/elder ....

Warm up

Name the family members.

A **family** is a group of people living together. **Parents** and their children are members of a family.

Do it yourself

Paste pictures of your family members including yourself on a chart. Write one line about each of them and present it in class.

Our parents are our mother and father. Their parents are our **grandparents**. Our sisters and brothers are called **siblings**. A pet is also a part of the family.

Types of Families

A family can be big or small.

Parents and children living together make a **small family**.

▲ A small family

Parents, grandparents and children living together make a **large family**. Sometimes, an **uncle**, an **aunt** and their children also live with them. This family is called a **joint family**.

▲ A joint family

Fact quest

All family members share the same last name. It is called a surname.

Find out

Who is a cousin? How many cousins do you have?

Fun with Family

All the members of a family have fun together.

▲ Playing together

▲ Celebrating together

▲ Going out together

They enjoy at home by playing games and watching TV together. They celebrate festivals together. They go out for picnics, visit people and other places.

Family members love and care for each other.

Eco feat

Ask your family members to use cloth or paper bags in place of plastic bags.

uncle: the brother of your mother or father or the husband of your aunt; **aunt:** the sister of your mother or father or the wife of your uncle

Recall

- A family is a group of people living together.
- A family can be small or large.
- Family members love and care for each other.

Work out

A. Choose the correct answers.

1. The members of a family live .... (together/separately).
2. Surnames are the .... (first names/last names).
3. The members of a family have .... (juice/fun) together.
4. A family can be small or .... (big/little).

B. Match the columns.

1.	Small family	a.	Father's or mother's sister
2.	Uncle	b.	Mother's or father's parents
3.	Grandparents	c.	Parents and children
4.	Aunt	d.	Mother's or father's brother

C. Who does these activities for you in your family?

1. Buys you things ....
2. Gets you ready for school ....
3. Cleans the house ....
4. Helps you with homework ....

Think

Think about your family and name these members.

1. The most caring member ....
2. The best cook ....
3. The tallest member ....
4. The most fun-loving member ....

Life Skills and Values

Write your parents' mobile numbers.

1. Mother's number ....
2. Father's number ....

Enjoy

Make a 'My Family' poster.

Take five or six ice cream sticks. Draw the faces of your family members on these sticks. Paste the sticks on a sheet and pin it up.

Let us play the game of snakes and ladders to learn about good and bad habits. Watch out for the snakes!

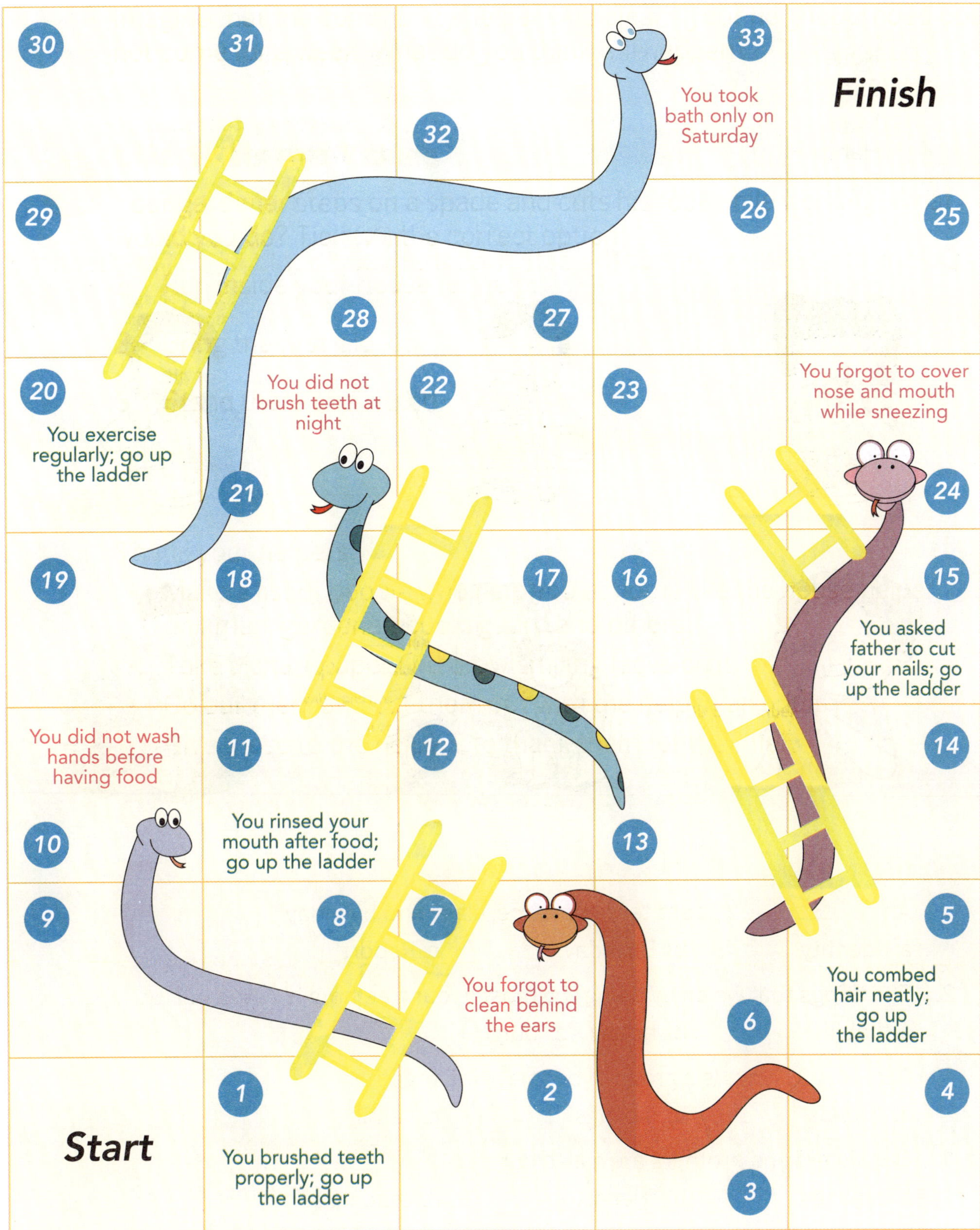

Worksheet (Chapters 1-4)

A. Match the organs with the actions.

1.	Nose	a.	Running
2.	Ears	b.	Drawing
3.	Legs	c.	Listening to music
4.	Hands	d.	Watching TV
5.	Eyes	e.	Smelling

B. Colour the boxes green for the activities that you should do to stay healthy.

C. Fill in the blanks with the correct answers.

1. An .... card tells our name, class and birthday
   a. Identity b. Birthday c. Report
2. The things that we enjoy doing the most in our free time is called our ....
   a. habit b. hobby c. duty
3. A .... is a group of people living together.
   a. friends b. siblings c. family
4. Our sisters and brothers are called our ....
   a. siblings b. friends c. teachers
5. Parents and children living together make a .... family.
   a. joint b. small c. large

5 School is Fun

Take off

- I go to school in ....
- I like to .... in school.

Warm up

What do you like to do in school?

We learn to read, write and count in school. We also learn to draw, play and sing. We wear a **uniform** when we go to school.

In the Classroom

▲ In a classroom

We study in a **classroom**. There are many classrooms in a school. A classroom has many desks and chairs, display boards and a blackboard or a white board. We follow rules in the classroom.

We listen to our teachers. We raise our hands for our turn to speak. We do not **litter** our classroom.

Eco feat

Keep a plant near a window in your class and take turns to water it.

---

litter: to make a place dirty

Do it yourself

Tick the things that you do in school.

 ☐

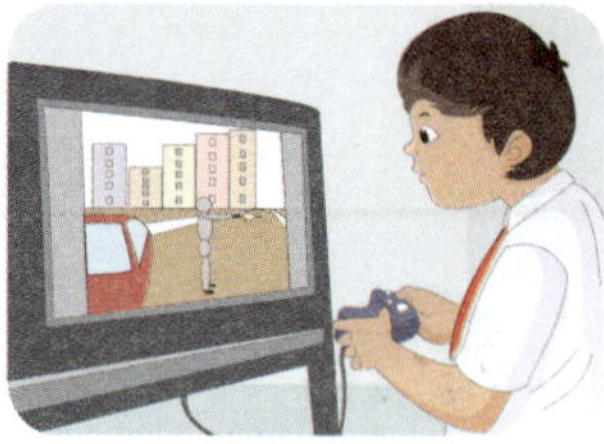 ☐

 ☐

 ☐

Other Places in School

A school has different places to do various activities.

We play in the school **playground**.

We go to the library to read and **borrow** books.

We go to the **computer lab** to learn about computers.

We go to the **music room** to learn music.

borrow: to take and use something that belongs to someone else and return it later

We eat lunch in the school **canteen**.

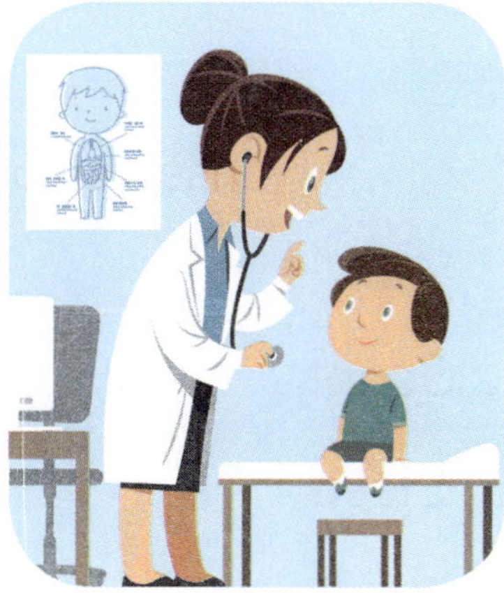

We go to the **medical room** if we feel unwell.

All schools have an office. The school **principal**, who is the head of the school, also has his or her own office. School functions are held in the **auditorium**.

We greet our teachers every day and learn to be **polite**.

We have many friends in school. We learn to share things with them.

We love our school. We should take care of our school and keep it clean.

▲ Principal

Fact quest

A boarding school is a place where students live and study.

Recall

- In school, we learn to read, write, count, draw, sing and work together.
- There are different places in a school to do various activities.
- We should keep our school clean.

polite: to speak softly with respect

Work out

A. Colour the box green for the activities you do in school.

1. Count ☐
2. Sleep ☐
3. Read ☐
4. Draw ☐
5. Watch TV ☐
6. Write ☐

B. Choose the correct word from the box and name the pictures.

classroom	library	playground
computer lab	music room	

....

....

....

....

....

C. Help Ria's grandmother drop Ria to school using the correct path. Colour the school too.

Think

How do you go to school? Is this mode of transport good for the environment?

Life Skills and Values

Tick (✓) the things you take to school in your school bag.

 ☐  ☐  ☐  ☐

 ☐  ☐  ☐  ☐

Enjoy

On a sheet of paper, list five actions that you should do and should not do in a classroom. Decorate the sheet with drawings.

Respect for School

We must respect our school by taking care of the places and the things we use in the school. We should also respect the people in our school. We must take care of our classmates.

We should not write on the library books or tear their pages.

We should put things back after using them.

We should throw trash in the dustbin.

We should not **scribble** on walls, desks and chairs in the classroom.

We should not pluck flowers or break the plants growing in the school.

We should wait for our turn while playing in the playground.

We should clean the blackboard and **arrange** the chairs in our classroom to keep it clean.

We should decorate our classroom.

We should respect our teachers.

scribble: to write something quickly; **arrange:** to plan or organize something

6 Places Around Us

Take off

▶ My address is ....
....
....
....

Warm up

Do you have a park near your house?

The people who live near our house are our **neighbours**. The area around our house is called a **neighbourhood**. There are many places in a neighbourhood, like a park, a school, a hospital, a post office and a market.

Find out

Who lives near your house?

We play in our neighbourhood **park**. Playing in the park helps us stay fit and healthy.

▲ Playing in a park

▲ Visiting a doctor

When we are ill, we visit a doctor in a clinic or **hospital** in the neighbourhood.

A **post office** helps us send letters and cards to our family and friends who live far away.

▲ At the post office

---

park: a place where people play, walk and relax

A **police station** is an important part of our neighbourhood. Police officers protect us from thieves.

▲ **A police station**

Fact quest

India has the largest number of post offices in the world.

Sometimes, there is a **school** in our neighbourhood. In school, we learn many things.

▲ **A school**

▲ **A neighbourhood**

A neighbourhood also has a **market** with many shops. We buy fruits and vegetables from a **greengrocer**.

We go to a **restaurant** to eat. We keep our money safe in a **bank**.

Eco feat

Always eat properly and do not waste food in a restaurant.

Do it yourself

Where would these people go to get their work done? Name the places.

1. Gurpreet should buy apples from a ....
2. Uncle Sunil wants to keep his money safe. He should go to a ....
3. Mrs Rai is feeling sick. She should go to a ....

greengrocer: a person who sells fruits and vegetables

A Good Neighbourhood

A good neighbourhood has all the places that we need. We should keep our neighbourhood clean. We should be kind and helpful to our neighbours.

Recall

- People who live near our house are our neighbours.
- The area around our house is called our neighbourhood.
- We have different places in a neighbourhood.

Work out

A. Choose the correct word from the box and fill in the blanks.

park	neighbourhood	clinic	neighbours

1. A .... is the area around our house.
2. People who live in the same neighbourhood are called ....
3. We go to a .... to play and walk.
4. We go to a doctor's .... when we fall sick.

B. Colour the box green if you see the following in your neighbourhood.

☐

☐

☐

☐

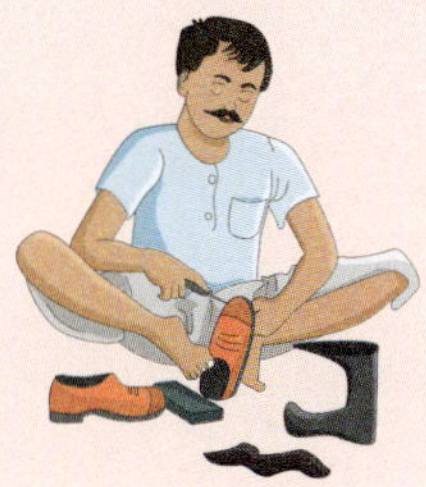

☐

Think

Think of any three ways in which you can help your neighbours.

Life Skills and Values

Your neighbour has asked you to help him fill some buckets of water from your house. What would you do?

1. Watch TV and not fill the buckets. ☐
2. Fill the buckets and ask your sibling to help you. ☐
3. Ask your helper to do it. ☐

Enjoy

Do you know your way around your neighbourhood? Draw a map of how to reach your house from the nearest market.

7 Helping Hands

Take off

- A .... treats me when I am not well.
- We buy fruits from the ....

Warm up

Who cleans your home? What do you think would happen if that person is not around?

There are many people who help us in our daily lives. They help us with the things that we cannot do ourselves. They help us at home, in school and in our neighbourhood. They are our **community helpers**.

Eco feat

A gardener takes care of plants and flowers. Plants and flowers keep the air clean.

A **cobbler** **mends** our shoes.

A **teacher** teaches us to read and write.

A **doctor** takes care of us when we are sick.

---

mend: to fix something broken

A **tailor** stitches our clothes.

A **hairdresser** cuts our hair.

A **traffic police officer** checks traffic.

A **carpenter** makes tables and chairs.

A **bus driver** takes us to school and brings us back home.

A **firefighter** puts out fires.

A **farmer** grows crops for us.

A **plumber** fixes pipes and taps.

A **sweeper** sweeps the street to keep it clean.

Fact quest

Even animals have people who help them. A doctor who treats animals is called a veterinarian.

Find out

What are the emergency numbers to call the police and the fire station?

Do it yourself

Read this rhyme and answer the questions.

Cobbler, Cobbler, what do you do?
I mend your shoes and polish them too.

Gardener, Gardener, what do you do?
I help keep your garden green under the sky so blue.

Barber, Barber, what do you do?
I cut your hair and style it too.

1. What does a cobbler use to polish our shoes?
2. What does the gardener use to keep our garden beautiful?
3. What does a barber use to cut our hair?

Community helpers help us live a **comfortable** life. We should be thankful to them and treat them with respect. Just as helpers help us, we too should try to help the people around us.

Recall

- Many people help us at home, in school and in the neighbourhood.
- We should be thankful to them and treat them with respect.

Work out

A. Fill in the blanks with the correct answers.

1. A .... makes chairs for us.
   a. gardener   b. carpenter
2. A .... mends our shoes.
   a. cobbler   b. pilot

comfortable: relaxed and free from worry

3. A .... grows crops for us.
   a. farmer   b. baker
4. A .... teaches us how to read and write.
   a. barber   b. teacher
5. A .... stitches our clothes.
   a. gardener   b. tailor

B. Match the people to the things they use.

1. 
2. 
3. 
4. 

a. 
b. 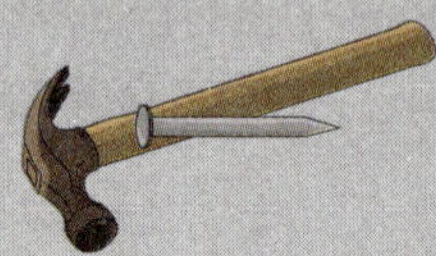
c. 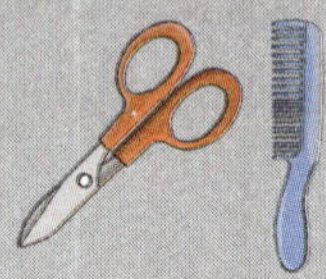
d. 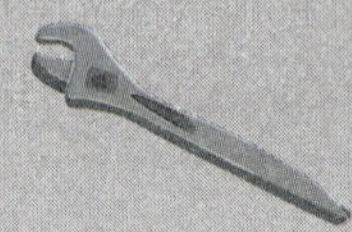

C. Solve these riddles and find out about some other helpers.

1. I fly a plane to help you travel to a different city or country.

   I am a P ...... L .... (LITPO)

2. I bake tasty cakes and cookies for you.

   I am a B .... E R. (KABRE)

3. I help the doctor take care of you when you are sick.

   I am a N ...... R .... (SUREN)

4. I deliver your cards, letters and parcels to your house.

   I am a P .... T...... A N. (PSOTNAM)

Think

Imagine that the community helper who cleans your neighbourhood does not come for a week. What do you think will happen?

Life Skills and Values

Your gardener steps on a spade and cuts his foot while working. What would you do? Tick (✓) the correct option.

1. Run inside your house for help. ☐
2. Bring the first-aid kit. ☐
3. Stand there and watch. ☐

Enjoy

Thank your helpers!

- Make a list of people who help you at home like the house helper, milkman, gardener, cook, guard and others.
- Take a chart paper and draw smiling faces on it.
- Colour them and cut them out with the help of an adult.
- Give these to the helpers to thank them for their help.

8 Houses Around Us

Take off

- I live with my family in a ....
- A house has many ....

Warm up

What is the home of a bird called?

We live with our family in a house. This house is called a **home**. Our home protects us from rain, wind, cold, heat, wild animals and thieves.

Types of Houses

There are many kinds of houses. Some are small and some are big. Houses that are made of mud, bamboo and straw are called *kutcha* houses. Houses made of bricks, cement and steel are called *pucca* houses.

▲ Kutcha house

▲ Pucca house

In a House

A house has different rooms for different activities.

It has **bedrooms** for sleeping, a **kitchen** for cooking food and a **bathroom** for bathing and washing.

It has a **dining room** for having breakfast, lunch and dinner with family.

Find out

Which kind of house do you live in—*kutcha* or *pucca*?

It has a **living room** to sit with friends and **guests**.

We should keep our homes neat and clean. We should also open the windows to let fresh air and sunlight in.

Eco feat

We should keep plants near windows and in balconies as they make the air clean.

Do it yourself

Label the rooms in a house.

Recall

- A house protects us from heat, cold and rain.
- There are many kinds of houses.
- A house is called a home when we live with our family.
- A house has different rooms for different activities.
- We should keep our homes neat and clean.

guests: people who have been invited to your house

Work out

A. Write in which room we find these things.

1. Bed: .... Stove: ....
2. Study table: .... TV: ....
3. Dining table: .... Shower: ....

B. Match the columns.

1. Kitchen	a. For sitting with guests
2. Bedroom	b. For bathing and washing
3. Bathroom	c. For resting and sleeping
4. Living room	d. For cooking food

C. Fill in the blanks.

1. A house is called a .... when we live with our family.
2. The two kinds of houses are .... and ....
3. A .... is a room used for eating meals with the family.
4. We should keep our homes .... and ....

Think

Every household has a set of rules that need to be followed. Make a list of three rules you should follow to make your house safe and comfortable. Remember to follow them at home.

....

....

....

Life Skills and Values

Tick (✓) the things you would do to keep your home clean.

Enjoy

On a chart paper, draw your house. Colour it in the same colours as your house. Next to it, draw your family members. Display your chart in class.

Look at the untidy room. Clean the room by joining things to their proper places in the second picture. One has been done for you.

Worksheet (Chapters 5-8)

A. Look at the pictures and name them using the help box.

Tailor	Post Office	Library	Firefighter	Music Room	Park

....

....

....

....

....

....

B. Fill in the blanks.

1. A .... mends our shoes.
2. School functions are held in the ....
3. A doctor works in a ....
4. We buy fruits and vegetables from a ....
5. We sit with our friends and guests in our ....

C. Write T for true and F for false.

1. We should respect our teachers. ☐
2. *Kutcha* houses are made of cement and bricks. ☐
3. We should not keep our neighbourhood clean. ☐
4. A post office helps us send letters and cards. ☐
5. A carpenter fixes pipes and taps. ☐

WORKSHEET

9 Food and Clothes

Take off

- I .... when I am hungry.
- We wear .... to cover our body.

Warm up

- Which is healthier of the two?
- What is the girl wearing that protects her from getting wet?

Food is important for all of us. We need food to live, grow and stay healthy. Food also gives us energy to work and play.

Food We Eat

We eat different kinds of food items. They are fruits, vegetables, grains, meat and milk products.

Fact quest

Water is just as important as food. We should drink six to eight glasses of water every day.

We get fruits, vegetables and grains from plants. We get milk, meat and eggs from animals.

Meals We Have

In a day, we have three **meals**. We eat **breakfast** in the morning, **lunch** in the afternoon and **dinner** at night. Breakfast is the most important meal of the day. We also eat **snacks** between breakfast and lunch, and again between lunch and dinner.

---

meal: food that we eat at a particular time; **snacks:** small amounts of food eaten between meals

▲ Breakfast

▲ Lunch

▲ Dinner

Do it yourself

Match the food groups with their names.

1. 
2. 
3. 
4. 
5. 

a. Vegetables
b. Milk products
c. Meat
d. Grains
e. Fruits

Good Food Habits

We should eat healthy meals. In order to stay fit, we should eat every type of food. Some food items that are not healthy are called **junk food**.

We should always eat fresh and clean food.

Find out

Which vegetables can be eaten without being cooked?

Clothes

Clothes cover our body. They protect us from heat, cold and rain. They also keep us safe from insect bites, dust and dirt.

junk food: food items that are not healthy

Different Clothes

We wear different kinds of clothes in different seasons. We wear light, **cotton** clothes when it is hot. Cotton clothes keep our body cool.

Fact quest

Leaves, animal fur and skin were the first types of clothing used.

▲ Cotton clothes keep our body cool

We wear **woollen** clothes to keep our body warm when it is cold. Woollen clothes are made of wool.

▲ Woollen clothes keep us warm

▲ Wear raincoat when it rains

When it rains, we wear raincoats, gumboots and carry umbrellas. Raincoats are made of rubber or plastic that does not get wet. We also wear rubber shoes called **gumboots** that are fit for the rainy season.

Eco feat

The cotton plant gives fibre for cotton clothes and its seeds are used as food for animals.

Uniforms

Sometimes a group of people wear special clothes. These are known as **uniforms**. We too wear uniforms to school.

▲ We wear uniforms to school

Find out

Which clothes do we wear when we go swimming?

cotton: clothes that are made from the cotton plant; **woollen:** clothes that are made from wool

Recall

- Food gives us energy to live, grow, work and play.
- We have three meals in a day—breakfast, lunch and dinner.
- We should eat healthy meals.
- Clothes protect us from heat, cold, rain and insect bites.
- We wear different clothes in different seasons.
- We sometimes wear special clothes to work called uniform.

Work out

A. Circle the food items that you like.

B. Write T for true and F for false.

1. We should not eat food properly. ☐
2. Food keeps us healthy. ☐
3. Food gives us energy. ☐
4. We should eat meals at any time of the day. ☐
5. We have breakfast at night. ☐

C. Fill in the blanks.

1. We wear clothes to protect us from .... and ....

2. Clothes are made up of .... and ....
3. Silk and woollen clothes keep us ....
4. .... and .... are worn to keep us dry during rains.

Think

A. What happens when you feel hungry and the food made at home is not something that you like? Should you eat only the food items that you like?

B. Name any three things that a tailor would use to make clothes.

....

Life Skills and Values

You wake up late every morning and always get late for school. So, you always miss your breakfast. What should you do?

1. Start waking up early. ☐
2. Keep waking up late. ☐
3. Eat breakfast anyway and reach late to school. ☐

Enjoy

Plate up your food in a drawing!

- On a chart paper, draw a circle. This will be your plate.
- On that plate, draw the food items that you like to eat. Remember to draw a little bit of every food type.
- Colour the food items and display the chart in class.

Good Food Habits

We should eat fresh food. Food eaten in the right amount is **healthy food**.

We should chew our food well and slowly.

We should not overeat.

We should eat slowly.

We must eat food that is covered.

We must always wash our hands before and after eating.

We should drink six to eight glasses of water every day.

We should never waste or throw food.

10 Let Us Celebrate

Take off

- I celebrate .... with my family and friends.
- We eat good .... and have fun during festivals.

Warm up

Talk about this picture in class.

We celebrate special days with our family and friends. Birthdays, weddings and festivals are **special days**.

Name two special days that you celebrate with your family.

....

▲ Celebrating birthday

A **festival** is a special time that we celebrate every year with family and friends. We wear new clothes, eat special food and **exchange** gifts and sweets with each other.

In India, we celebrate different festivals. Some festivals are celebrated only by certain groups of people, while others are celebrated by everyone.

---

exchange: doing or giving something to someone in return for something else

Diwali

▲ Celebrating Diwali

Diwali is known as the the 'Festival of Lights'. On this day, people pray and make rangoli to **decorate** their homes. They light *diyas* and candles, make sweets and invite friends and relatives for a **feast**.

Eco feat

Bursting crackers makes the air dirty.

Christmas

Christmas is celebrated on 25 December as the birthday of Jesus Christ. People go to church to pray on this day. They decorate their homes with a Christmas tree, make cakes and exchange gifts with family and friends.

▲ Celebrating Christmas

▲ Celebrating Gurpurab

Gurpurab

On **Gurpurab**, people celebrate Guru Nanak's birthday. On this day, people pray in a gurudwara. They eat langar which is a community meal together.

Eid-ul-Fitr

Eid-ul-Fitr is another festival celebrated in India. On this day, people go to a mosque to pray. A special sweet dish called *seviyan* is prepared on this day. People have a **grand** feast with friends and relatives.

▲ Celebrating Eid

Find out

Which festivals do your classmates celebrate?

decorate: to make something look good by putting nice things on it; **feast:** a special meal eaten together to celebrate special days; **grand:** large and important

Do it yourself

Match the picture to its name.

1. 

2. 

3. 

4. 

a. Temple b. Church c. Mosque d. Gurudwara

▲ Republic Day parade

All Indians celebrate three special days known as **national festivals**.

Independence Day is celebrated on 15 August every year as India became a free country on this day.

Republic Day is celebrated on 26 January each year. India became a **republic** on this day.

Gandhi Jayanti is celebrated on 2 October every year. On this day, Mahatma Gandhi was born.

Fact quest

The first president of India was Dr Rajendra Prasad.

Recall

- A festival is a special time that we celebrate every year with family and friends.
- Diwali, Eid, Christmas and Gurpurab are some of the festivals that we celebrate.
- Independence Day, Republic Day and Gandhi Jayanti are national festivals.

republic: a country that is governed by a president and politicians elected by the people, and where there is no king or queen

Work out

A. Match the pictures to their names.

1. 

a. Christmas

2. 

b. Republic Day

3. 

c. Diwali

4. 

d. Gurpurab

B. Look at the pictures and identify the festival related to it.

....

....

....

C. Fill in the blanks.

1. The festival celebrating the birthday of Guru Nanak is called ....
2. .... is also known as the Festival of Lights.
3. .... is a special dish prepared during Eid.
4. India became a republic on ....
5. Gandhi Jayanti is celebrated on .... every year.

Think

Why do dogs run away when people burst crackers during festivals?

Life Skills and Values

Your neighbours have invited your family to celebrate their festival with them. What would you do?

1. Share their celebrations ☐
2. Understand and appreciate their festival ☐
3. Make an excuse and not go to your neighbour's house ☐

Enjoy

Paper rangoli

- Take a piece of paper and fold it two times.
- Take a pair of scissors and with the help of an elder, cut out small designs. You can even use a hole puncher.
- Make sure the folds are joined while cutting out the design or punching in the holes. Open the page. Your paper *rangoli* is ready!

11 Ways We Travel

Take off

- I go to school by ....
- A bicycle has .... wheels.
- A .... helps us cross rivers and lakes.

Warm up

Which of these vehicles have you travelled on?

We **travel** when we go from one place to another. We use different ways to travel. The different **means of transport** take us from one place to another. We travel to school, to work, to the market or for vacations.

Find out

What is a cable car? Does it have wheels?

▲ Fast and slow vehicles

We use different kinds of **vehicles** to travel. Most vehicles run on wheels, like cars and buses. Vehicles that travel on water do not run on wheels.

Vehicles can be **fast** or **slow**. A rickshaw, a cycle and a bullock cart move slowly. A car, a bus, a train, a metro and an aeroplane move fast.

---

means of transport: the different ways by which we travel such as land, air, water; **vehicles:** machines that take people from one place to another

Ways We Travel

Vehicles move on land, air or water.

We use vehicles like cars, cycles, buses and trains to **travel by land**.

Eco feat

Motor vehicles give off smoke, which makes the air dirty. We should walk or cycle more.

▲ Travel by land

In some villages, bullock carts are also used to travel short distances. Roads and railway tracks are built to help us travel on land.

We use boats, ships and other kinds of vehicles to **travel by water**.

We use an aeroplane, a helicopter and a hot air balloon to **travel by air**.

▲ Travel by water

Many people going to the same place can travel together.

Fact quest

Rockets are tall and round spacecrafts that are used to travel to space.

▲ Travel by air

Recall

- We often go from one place to another for different work. This is called travelling.
- We travel by land, water and air to go to different places.
- We use different kinds of vehicles to travel.

Work out

A. Fill in the blanks with the correct answers.

1. A .... is a vehicle.
   a. bus   b. air   c. road
2. A .... can be used to travel short distances.
   a. cycle rickshaw   b. train   c. helicopter
3. A .... is mostly used in villages.
   a. bullock cart   b. ship   c. aeroplane

B. Draw and colour your favourite vehicle.

C. Write the number of wheels each vehicle has.

☐ ☐ ☐ ☐ ☐

Think

You and your neighbourhood friend go to the same school. Yet, you travel in different cars. Do you think this is right? What do you think you should do?

Life Skills and Values

What should we use to wash our cars?

1. Water from the hosepipe ☐
2. Water in a bucket ☐

Discuss the answers in the class.

Enjoy

Make your own sailboat.

You will need paper, a drinking straw, a round plastic lid and play dough.

1. Cut out a coloured sheet of paper in the shape of a triangle and decorate it.
2. Make three holes on its straight side. This would be your mast.
3. Take a drinking straw and weave it through the holes.
4. Now, take a round plastic lid and place a ball of play dough on it.
5. Fix the straw in the play dough and your sail boat is ready. The boat can also float in water.

12 Be Safe

Take off

- I should .... (play/not play) with knives.
- I should .... (not talk/talk) to people I don't know.

Warm up

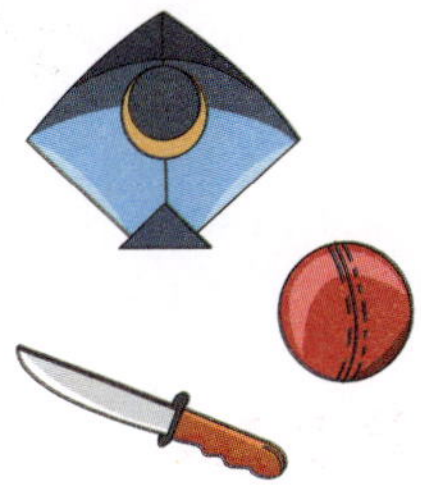

Are all these things safe to play with?

Safety means to protect ourselves from danger or harm. We should always be careful and safe.

In order to be safe, we need to follow certain rules. These rules help us to avoid **accidents**. If we do not follow safety rules, we can hurt not only ourselves, but others too.

Being Safe at Home

▲ Use scissors with an adult

- Do not play with sharp things like scissors and knives as they might hurt us. If you do, ask an adult to help you.
- Do not play with electrical switches and plugs.
- Do not open the door to **strangers**.
- Do not take medicines without taking permission from elders or a doctor.
- Do not go near the gas stove, oven or iron as we might get burnt from them.
- Do not play with matchsticks and candles.

---

accident: an event that happens suddenly causing people harm; **strangers:** people you do not know

Do it yourself

Circle the sharp things that we should not play with.

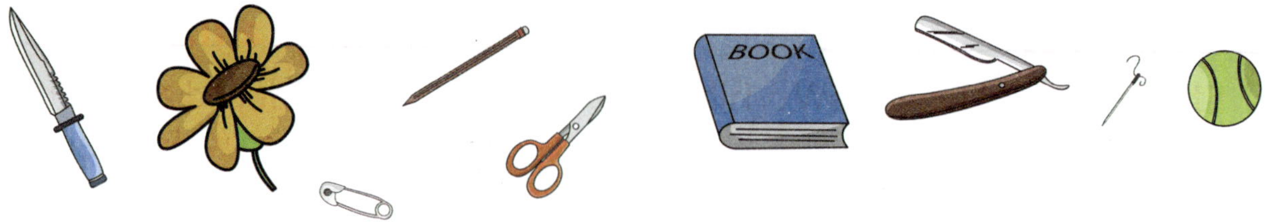

Being Safe on the Road

Fact quest

The red light says 'stop'.
The yellow light says 'wait'.
The green light says 'go'.

- Always wait for the light to turn red and the traffic to stop before crossing the road.
- Always look at both sides of the road before crossing.
- Cross the road only at the **zebra crossing**.
- While walking on the road, always walk on the **footpath**.
- While travelling on a car or a bus, never put your hands or head out of the window.
- Always wear a seatbelt while travelling by car.

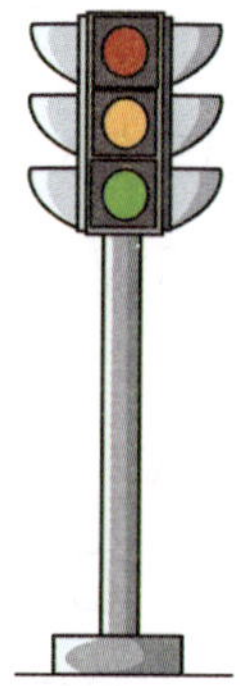

Now, read this rhyme about crossing the road.

Stop, look and listen,

before you cross the street.

First use your eyes and ears,

then use your feet.

▲ Crossing a road

zebra crossing: an area on the road painted with white stripes; **footpath:** a narrow path for walking

Being Safe at School

- Do not jump on desks and chairs.
- Do not push anyone while walking or climbing the stairs.
- Always stand in a queue while **boarding** and getting off a bus.
- In the playground, do not stand in front of swings or jump off seesaws.

▲ Standing in a queue

We must keep a first-aid kit at home, in school and in the car. **First aid** is the first help given to someone who is injured.

Find out

What things does a first-aid box have?

Recall

- We should always be careful and take care of ourselves.
- We should protect ourselves from danger and harm to avoid accidents.
- To be safe, we must follow certain rules.
- We should follow the safety rules at home, on the road and in school.

Work out

A. Choose the correct answers.

1. I .... (do/do not) play in the kitchen.
2. I .... (do/do not) put my finger in an electrical socket.
3. I play in the .... (park/road).
4. The red traffic light means .... (go/stop).

boarding: to get on to a bus or any other vehicle

B. Write **Y** for the correct action and **N** for the wrong action.

C. Fill in the blanks.

1. .... means to protect ourselves from danger or harm.
2. Do not .... the door to strangers.
3. Always cross on the .... crossing.
4. .... is the first help given to an injured person.

Think

Is this safe? Talk about it in class.

Life Skills and Values

If your brother falls down and hurts himself, tick (✓) what you would do.

1. Help him to get up.
2. Start crying.
3. Tell an adult to come and help.

Enjoy

Make a first-aid box with the help of your parents. Put all the things that should be kept in a first-aid box. Keep it at your home.

Play the game 'Trek to your holiday home'. Roll the dice and move your button. Follow the instructions.

WORKSHEET

Worksheet (Chapters 9-12)

A. Write any two things that you eat for these meals.

1. Breakfast ....
2. Lunch ....
3. Dinner ....

B. Write the name of the festival below each picture.

....

C. Write L for land transport, W for water transport and A for air transport vehicles.

1.  ☐
2.  ☐
3.  ☐
4.  ☐
5.  ☐
6.  ☐

D. Write Yes or No.

1. We must follow rules at home. ....
2. We must play on the road. ....
3. We should not open doors for strangers. ....
4. We must stand in a line while boarding the bus. ....

13 Plants Around Us

Take off

- Plants need .... to grow.
- Some plants are big and some are ....

Warm up

Talk about the plants you see in the picture.

Plants are all around us. We find them in gardens, in forests and even by the road. They are **living things**.

Fact quest

Plants need air, water, sunlight and soil. They can make their own food.

Types of Plants

Plants are different in shape, size and colour. Some are big and some are small.

Plants that are big and tall are called **trees**. They have a strong, thick stem called **trunk**.

▲ Mango tree

Shrubs are the plants that are taller than herbs and shorter than trees. They have many branches and **woody** stems.

▲ Shrub

Short plants with soft, green stems are called **herbs**.

living things: things that live and grow; **woody:** thick, hard and wood-like

▲ Coriander is a herb

Some plants cannot stand straight and need some **support** to climb. They are called **climbers**.

▲ Grapevine is a climber

Some plants **creep** on the ground. They are called **creepers**. As their fruits are big and heavy, they spread their branches on the ground.

▲ Pumpkin is a creeper

Look at the picture of the plant and read the names of its parts.

▲ Parts of a plant

Eco feat

Trees are cut down to make paper. Therefore, we should not waste paper.

Uses of Plants

Plants are very useful to us.

- They keep the air we breathe fresh and clean.
- They give us food like fruits, vegetables, grains and leaves.
- They give us wood that is used to make tables and chairs.

support: to help something; **creep:** to move slowly

- They give us materials like cotton and jute that are used to make clothes and bags.
- They give us medicines.

We should plant more trees and take care of them.

Do it yourself

Circle the things that we get from plants.

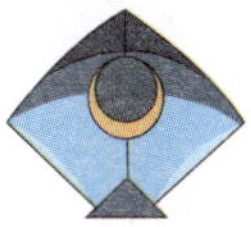

Recall

- Plants are living things.
- There are different kinds of plants.
- These are trees, herbs, shrubs, climbers and creepers.
- Plants are very useful to us.

Work out

A. Look at the pictures. Tick the correct answers to name the type of these plants.

1. 

   a. Climber b. Herb

2. 

   a. Creeper b. Shrub

3. 

a. Tree b. Climber

B. Match the columns.

1.	Tree	a.	Short plants with soft green stems
2.	Herb	b.	Takes support to grow upwards
3.	Shrub	c.	Grows along the ground
4.	Creeper	d.	Shorter than trees and taller than herbs
5.	Climber	e.	Strong thick trunk

C. Colour and name the plants.

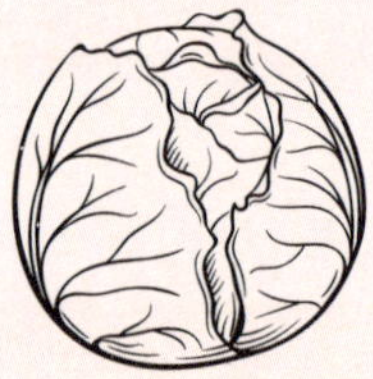

....

....

....

Think

How do we use the different parts of a plant?

Life Skills and Values

Imagine you are a plant and someone wants to adopt you. Write a list of instructions for your new owner, explaining how he or she should care for you.

Enjoy

Collect a few leaves of different kinds and sizes. Press them in a heavy book for a week in order to dry them. When the leaves become dry, paste them on paper to make greeting cards.

14 Animals Around Us

Take off

- We keep some animals in our homes. We call them ....
- An animal that lives in the jungle is a ....

Warm up

Which animal do you see in the picture

We can see many animals around us. Some animals are big and some are small. Birds, fish and insects are types of animals too.

Types of Animals

Some **domestic** animals live with us in our homes. They are like our friends. We call them **pets**. Dogs, cats, and fish are some animals we keep as pets. We love and take care of our pets.

▲ Pets

domestic: not wild, kept at home or on a farm; **pets:** animals we keep at home

We keep some animals near our homes or on a farm as they are useful to us. We call them **domestic animals**. Horses, cows, buffaloes, camels and goats are some domestic animals.

▲ Domestic animals

Some animals live in forests. They are called **wild animals**. Lions, tigers, crocodiles and bears are some wild animals.

▲ **Wild animals**

Do it yourself

Join the dots to draw a big and a small animal and colour them.

Food for Animals

▲ Giraffe

Like human beings, animals also need food to live and grow. Different animals eat different kinds of food.

Fact quest

Plant-eating animals are called **herbivores** and flesh-eating animals are called **carnivores**.

Animals like cows, goats, sheep, horses, elephants, giraffes and rabbits eat plants, fruits and vegetables. Animals like tigers, lions, foxes, eagles, cheetahs and wolves eat the flesh of other animals.

Animals like bears, crows, dogs and cats eat both plants and the flesh of other animals.

Baby animals get their food from their mothers.

Animal Homes

Different animals have different kinds of homes to protect themselves from rain, cold, heat and wind.

Eco feat

Many animals are killed to make leather from their skin.

Birds make **nests**.

We keep fish in an **aquarium**.

A cow lives in a **shed**.

A horse lives in a **stable**.

A lion lives in a **den**.

A rabbit lives in a **burrow**.

Animals Help Us

Animals help us in many ways. Cows, goats and buffaloes give us milk. Sheeps give us wool and bees give us honey.

▲ We must look after the animals

Recall

- Pets live with us in our homes.
- Domestic animals are useful to us.
- Wild animals live in forests.
- Animals need food to live and to grow.

Work out

A. Write the type of the animals given here.

1.    ....

2.    ....

3.    ....

B. Match the animals and their homes.

1.	Dog	b.	Burrow
2.	Birds	c.	Kennel
3.	Lion	d.	Den
4.	Horse	e.	Nest
5.	Rabbit	f.	Stable

C. Write T for true and F for false.

1. Lion is a wild animal. ☐
2. Horse is a domestic animal. ☐
3. Cat is a pet animal. ☐
4. Goats give us eggs. ☐

Think

In zoos, animals are kept in cages. Do you think animals are happy there?

Life Skills and Values

Solve these riddles.

1. I am the king of the jungle. .... (OINL)
2. I have a long trunk. .... (LEEPAHTN)
3. I am the tallest animal in the jungle. .... (FFGRIAE)
4. I am the fastest animal. .... (AHCEETH)

Enjoy

Make your own paper pet dog.

Fold a square paper as instructed.

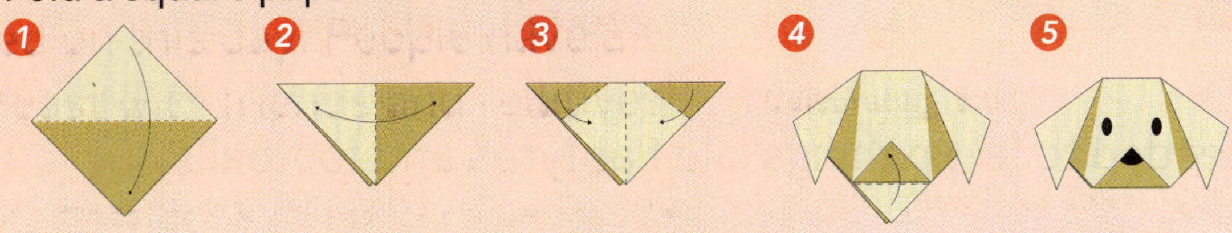

15 Air and Water

Take off

- All living things need .... to breathe.
- We need to drink six to eight glasses of .... every day.

Warm up

What do you blow into a balloon?

Air is all around us. We cannot see air but we feel it. We feel air when leaves rustle and when the fan gives a cool effect.

Air moves from one place to another. Moving air is called **wind**. When air moves softly, it is called a **breeze**. At times, the wind blows strongly. It is called a **storm**.

Need for Air

Try pinching your nose for a few seconds. Does that make you feel uneasy?

We need air to breathe and live.

Air is useful in many ways.

Eco feat

We should plant more trees. Trees make the air clean.

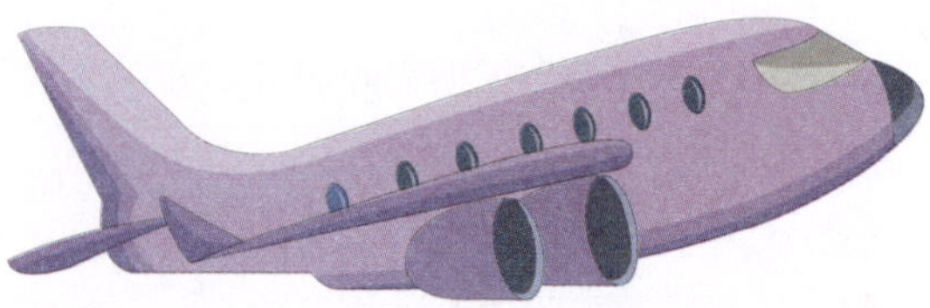

Air helps things like kites and aeroplanes to fly.

Air is needed to fill up things like flat tyres and footballs.

Air helps in drying wet clothes.

Boats and windmills move with the help of air.

We need air to start a fire.

Can you think of some other uses of air?

Clean Air is Important

We should keep the air clean. Smoke and dust make the air dirty.

If we breathe dirty air, we fall sick.

▲ Smoke makes air dirty

Fact quest

When we blow air into water through a straw, we get bubbles. Bubbles are balls of air in water!

Eco feat

Do not waste water. Use only as much water as you need.

Water

We need water to live. Plants and animals also need water to live.

Water is used by us in many ways. We need water for drinking, bathing, cleaning and cooking. We also need water for putting out fires.

We use water for fun activities like swimming and surfing.

Animals and birds also need water to drink and to keep cool.

We get water from **oceans**, seas, rivers, lakes, **streams**, ponds, well and rain.

We have pipes and taps in our homes that help us get water.

▲ Well

▲ Sea

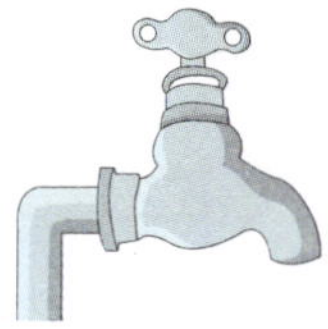

▲ Tap

▲ Stream

▲ Lake

▲ Pond

▲ Ocean

Clean Water

We should always drink clean water. Drinking dirty water can make us fall sick. Animals and birds too can fall sick if they drink dirty water.

Find out

Why should we not drink sea water?

We should never throw garbage into lakes, rivers and other **sources** of water.

Do it yourself

Circle the things that need air to move.

---

ocean: a very big amount of water in one place; **stream:** a small, narrow river; **sources:** a place, person or thing from which we get something

Recall

- Human beings, plants and animals need air and water to live.
- Air and water are useful in many ways.
- We should keep the air clean.
- We get water from many sources.
- Dirty water can make us fall sick.
- We should not waste water or make it dirty.

Work out

A. Look at the pictures and tick (✓) the things that need water.

 ☐

 ☐

 ☐

 ☐

B. Choose the correct answers.

1. We should .... (turn on/turn off) the taps after using them.
2. We should not drink .... (clean/dirty) water.
3. Water is .... (important/useless).
4. We get water in our homes with the help of .... (pipes/wells).
5. We need water for .... (cooking/breathing).

C. Tick the things that can be done to keep the air and water clean.

1. Burn leaves and crackers ☐
2. Plant trees ☐

3. Never throw garbage in a river, lake, or sea.

4. Walk for short distances

Think

Tick (✓) what you would do in this situation.

You see that one of the taps in your house is leaking.

a. Tell your parents immediately.

b. Try to fix it yourself.

c. Let it leak.

Life Skills and Values

Circle the people who are not dirtying the air.

Enjoy

A. Let us make a wind chime.

You will need five long sticks, five strings of equal length and one thick bangle.

1. Take the sticks and tie them to the strings.
2. Then tie the other end of the strings to the bangle.
3. Now tie a long string at the centre of the bangle for hanging.
4. Your wind chime is ready!

16 Earth and Sky

Take off

- The Earth is .... like a ball.
- I see .... and .... when I look at the night sky.

Warm up

What do you see when you look up at the day sky?

The Earth is our home. It is round like an orange. It is made up of **land** and **water**.

We live on land along with many plants and animals. Fish, whales, tortoises and other animals along with some plants live in water.

▲ Land

Land

Land has many shapes and forms. It can be flat or raised. A flat land is called a **plain**. A raised land is called a **hill**. A high hill is called a **mountain**.

Find out

Name some animals that live on land.

Water

Water on Earth is found in oceans, seas, lakes, rivers, ponds, springs, streams and waterfalls. In cold areas, water is found in the form of snow and ice.

▲ Snow and ice

Sky

What do we see when we look up?

The big open space above us is called the **sky**. It appears blue in the morning. We see the Sun and clouds in the sky during the day. The Sun gives light to the Earth.

Fact quest

The direction from where the Sun rises is called the east.

When the Sun sets, it becomes night. The sky appears black in the night. We see stars and the moon in the night sky.

▲ Day sky

▲ Night sky

Do it yourself

Look at these pictures. Write whether you see them at night or during the day.

....

....

....

Recall

- The Earth is made up of land and water.
- Land has many shapes and forms.
- The sky has clouds, stars, the Sun and the moon.

Work out

A. Fill in the blanks.

1. In cold areas, water is found in the form of .... and ....
2. .... and .... can be seen in the sky at night.
3. Earth has land and ....
4. A high hill is called a ....

B. Match the columns.

1. Fish	a. Plains
2. Sun	b. Snow
3. Water	c. Day
4. Clouds	d. Ocean
5. Flat land	e. Sky

C. Colour the picture given below.

Think

Why does the sky turn dark at night?

Life Skills and Values

Earth is beautiful, but we are making it dirty. We should keep the Earth clean. How can we keep it clean?

Enjoy

Make a stars-and-moon wall hanging.

1. Draw the moon and stars on a sheet of paper. Cut them out and colour them.
2. Then, tie them to strings.
3. Connect these strings to a long stick.
4. Your wall hanging is ready.

Help the four animals reach their homes.

WORKSHEET

Worksheet (Chapters 13-16)

A. Fill in the blanks.

1. We get .... and .... from animals.
2. Drinking .... water will make us sick.
3. We need .... to breathe and live.
4. .... have a strong, thick stem called trunk.
5. The Sun is high in the sky in the ....

B. Match the animals with the food that they like to eat.

1. 
2. 
3. 
4. 

a. 
b. 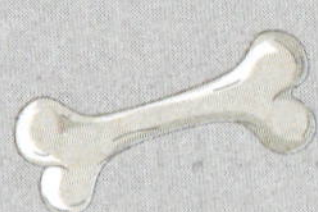
c. 
d. 

C. Tick (✓) the correct sentence.

1. Land has many forms. ☐
2. Air helps in drying wet clothes. ☐
3. We should never throw garbage in any source of water. ☐
4. Shrubs are taller than herbs and shorter than trees. ☐
5. The sun rises in the evening. ☐

D. Where do you see these things? Write L for land, S for sky and W for water.

 ☐
 ☐
 ☐
 ☐
 ☐
 ☐
 ☐
 ☐
 ☐